My Healthy Habits

EAT RIGHT
TO FUEL YOUR BODY

Norwood House Press

Madison Parker

Cataloging-in-Publication Data

Names: Parker, Madison.
Title: Eat right to fuel your body / Madison Parker.
Description: Buffalo, NY : Norwood House Press, 2026. | Series: My healthy habits | Includes glossary and index.
Identifiers: ISBN 9781978575318 (pbk.) | ISBN 9781978575325 (library bound) | ISBN 9781978575332 (ebook)
Subjects: LCSH: Nutrition--Juvenile literature. | Dietetics--Juvenile literature. | Food habits--Juvenile literature.
Classification: LCC RA784.P375 2026 | DDC 613.2--dc23

Published in 2026 by
Norwood House Press
2544 Clinton Street
Buffalo, NY 14224

Designer: Rhea Magaro
Editor: Kim Thompson

Photo credits: Cover, p. 1 Russamee/Shutterstock.com; p. 5 Volodymyr TVERDOKHLIB/Shutterstock.com; p. 7 Elena Eryomenko/Shutterstock.com; p. 8 GSDesign/Shutterstock.com; p. 9 PeopleImages.com Yuri A/Shutterstock.com; p. 10 Andreas Gradin/Shutterstock.com; p. 11 Adri Yadam Nasir/Shutterstock.com; p. 13 Vladislav Noseek/Shutterstock.com; p. 14 Joshua Resnick/Shutterstock.com; p. 15 henrique ferrera/Shutterstock.com; p. 16 Africa Studio/Shutterstock.com; p. 17 stockcreations/Shutterstock.com; p. 18 fizkes/Shutterstock.com; p. 19 Komuso and Colorsandia/Shutterstock.com; p. 21 Monkey Business Images

Printed in the United States of America

CPSIA compliance information: Batch #CSNHP26: For further information contact Norwood House Press at 1-800-237-9932.

TABLE OF CONTENTS

EATING HEALTHY IS IMPORTANT

Eating healthy foods makes your body strong. It makes you feel good. It provides the **energy** you need every day.

FOOD GROUPS ARE FUEL

Food is the **fuel** your body runs on. To stay healthy, eat foods from all the food groups. Include **protein**, dairy foods, whole grains, fruits, and vegetables.

Protein helps your body grow and repair **muscles**. It keeps you strong and active. **Lean** meats like chicken are full of protein. So are eggs, beans, and nuts.

Dairy foods help your body build strong bones and teeth. They include milk, cheese, and yogurt. These foods are full of **calcium**.

Foods made from whole grains provide energy that lasts all day. They include whole-wheat bread, oatmeal, and brown rice. These foods are full of **fiber**, which helps you feel full.

Fruits and vegetables are packed with vitamins and **nutrients**. They help your body protect itself and fight off sickness. Choose foods like apples, blueberries, carrots, spinach, and broccoli.

BALANCED MEALS

Balanced meals include foods from several food groups. A balanced breakfast gives you energy to start the day. Want a breakfast with whole grains, dairy, protein, and fruit? Have oatmeal with berries and a glass of milk. Add a slice of whole-grain toast with peanut butter.

For lunch, a mix of protein, vegetables, and whole grains will keep you feeling full and focused. Try a turkey sandwich on whole-wheat bread with lettuce and tomato.

Dinner is a good time to put a variety of foods on your plate. Try chicken, brown rice, and carrots. Add a side salad for extra veggies.

SNACKS AND TREATS

Healthy snacks give you extra energy between meals. Some good snacks are yogurt with sliced strawberries or a handful of nuts.

Occasional treats can be part of a healthy diet. When you have a treat, add in something healthy. Ice cream with fresh fruit is a sweet treat that includes extra vitamins.

DRINKING WATER

Water helps your muscles work. It makes your skin glow. It even helps you think more clearly. Drinking water every day keeps your body healthy.

To stay **hydrated**, choose water instead of sugary drinks. Drinking water at mealtimes and throughout the day is a great way to keep your body healthy.

HEALTHY AND STRONG

Eating right gives your body the fuel it needs. It helps you grow strong, stay healthy, and feel great! By choosing foods from each food group, you can give your body the energy it needs to work, play, and learn.

GLOSSARY

calcium (KAL-see-uhm): a mineral that is found in dairy foods and that is needed for strong teeth and bones

energy (EN-ur-jee): the strength to do things without getting tired

fiber (FYE-bur): parts of some foods, like whole grains, that help you feel full and that keep your stomach healthy

fuel (FYOO-uhl): a source of energy

hydrated (HYE-dray-tid): full of moisture; not dry

lean (leen): not fatty

muscles (MUHS-uhlz): the parts of your body that allow you to move

nutrients (NOO-tree-uhnts): parts of food, such as vitamins and minerals, that help your body grow and stay healthy

occasional (uh-KAY-zhuh-nuhl): sometimes, but not often

protein (PROH-teen): a nutrient that helps the body build muscle and that is found in foods such as meat, eggs, and beans

THINKING QUESTIONS

1. Why is it important to eat foods from all the food groups?
2. What foods are good sources of protein and how do they help your body?
3. How does drinking water help your body stay healthy?
4. Give examples of balanced meals for breakfast, lunch, and dinner.
5. How can you enjoy treats while still giving your body what it needs?

INDEX

ABOUT THE AUTHOR

Madison Parker spent her childhood in the city of Chicago, Illinois. A farm girl at heart, today she lives in Wisconsin with her husband and four children on a small farm with cows, goats, chickens, and two miniature horses named Harley and David. Her favorite dessert is vanilla frozen custard with rainbow sprinkles, even in the winter.